Visit us on the Web!
rhcbooks.com
www.sesamestreet.org

Educators and librarians, for a variety of teaching tools, visit us at RHTeachersLibrarians.com

ISBN 978-0-593-31009-0 (trade) — ISBN 978-0-593-31010-6 (ebook)

MANUFACTURED IN CHINA
10 9 8 7 6 5 4 3 2 1

Answers to Calm First-Day-of-School Jitters

By Sonali Fry

Illustrated by Joe Mathieu

Random House 🏠 New York

Dear Parents,

The first day of school can be exciting for your child, but it can also be filled with stress, as everything is new and different. Prepare your child by talking about their new school, their new teacher and classes, and the changes from their normal routine. Here are some things you can do to calm those nerves:

• Talk with your child about what to expect.

• Mention activities they might get to do, such as gym and art.

• If the school offers an open house, attend it with your child.

• Talk about the feelings your child might have, such as being scared, nervous, excited, happy, or sad. Let them know it's okay to feel that way.

- Involve your child in the preparations for the first day, such as making a list of school supplies, looking for new clothes, and possibly getting a new backpack.

- The night before, have them help pick out their first-day outfit.

- Select a special object for your child to take to school, such as a small stuffed toy or family photo.

- Tie a string around your wrist and a matching one around your child's, which they can touch when they need comfort.

- Plan a fun dinner, when you can hear all about their day and answer any questions they might have.

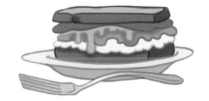

Your child's first day of school is a milestone moment you will treasure forever.

"Time for bed, Elmo!" called Elmo's mommy.
Elmo was playing with Baby David. He wasn't ready for bed!
"Why does Elmo have to go to bed?" he asked.
"Tomorrow is your first day of school, Elmo!" said Mommy.
"Remember how we set out your special outfit?"
Elmo's tummy felt funny.

Mommy hugged Elmo close. "It's okay to wonder about that. You will get to know everyone by talking to them and spending time with them, and you'll make so many new friends."

Prairie Dawn and her mom were out for a walk.
"Look—there's your new school," said Mom.
"Are you looking forward to your first day?"
Prairie Dawn stared at the building.
"What's wrong?" asked Mom.

Mom gave Prairie Dawn a big hug. "Your teacher will tell you where to sit. And that might be your special seat for the entire year."

Prairie Dawn smiled.

"I love story time with you, Granny," said Big Bird. "Can you read to me every day?"

"You're starting school tomorrow, so we'll have to wait to read together again," said Granny.

Big Bird felt sad.

What if . . . ? What if there are no books to read at school?

"There will be SO MANY books at school!" said Granny, smiling. "Books you've never read before, about animals, pirates, and even dinosaurs! And your teacher will read to you every day."

Big Bird thought for a bit.

"I like you reading to me best, Granny. But I'm excited to read new books, too."

Abby was helping her little brother, Rudy, get his backpack ready for school.

"Let's see," said Abby, looking in his pack. "You've got your crayons, folder, and lunch box."

Rudy looked in his backpack, too. What about his toys?

What if . . . ? What if I miss my favorite toy?

Abby put her arm around Rudy. "Don't worry, little brother! You can take your favorite toy with you!" she said. "But it has to stay in your backpack at school. I keep Prince in the front pouch of my backpack."

Rudy was relieved. He picked up his favorite stuffed dog and tucked it into his backpack.

"I can't wait to make new friends, play games, and learn new things!" said Rosita.

"Sounds like you're very excited about going to school," said Dad.

"Dinner is almost ready," called Rosita's mom. "Please go to the bathroom and wash your hands."

Rosita stopped smiling.

"*¿Qué pasa?* . . . What's wrong, Rosita?" asked Dad.

What if . . . ?
What if I don't
know where the
bathroom is?

Dad put his hand on Rosita's shoulder. "I used to worry about that, too! If you need to go to the bathroom, *mi amor,* just tell your teacher. She will show you where it is."

"*¡Excelente!*" said Rosita.

Abby Cadabby and her dad were in the community garden.
"Oopsie!" said Abby. "Oh, no!"
"What's wrong?" asked Dad.
"I put cucumber seeds in the squash patch," explained
Abby. She looked worried.

"Oh, honey, everyone makes mistakes," said Dad. "I make mistakes all the time."

"Really?" asked Abby.

"Sure," said Dad. "That's how you learn! I learn from my mistakes, and you will, too. Come on, let's dig up those cucumber seeds and put them where they belong."

Zoe was having an end-of-summer dance party!
"Your friends will be here any minute," said Zoe's dad.
Zoe smiled. "I love to dance! Can I dance at school?"
"You can dance during recess," said Mom. "That's when
you can play all kinds of games."

What if . . . ?
What if no one
wants to play
with me?

"I have an idea," said Mom. "You can watch what other kids are playing, and then add to it. If they're playing superheroes, what kind of superhero could *you* be?"

"I could be Super Dancer Girl!" said Zoe. "And I'd show them my super dance moves!"

Gabrielle was having lunch with her dad.
"Mmm . . . I love crunchy carrots," said Gabrielle.
"Tomorrow you'll be eating your carrots at school," said Pop.
Gabrielle stopped chomping.

Pop bit into his carrot with a *snap*.
"That's what snack time is for!" Pop said. "We will pack your lunch box full of yummy food. Then you can eat some at snack time."

Elmo's parents tucked him into bed.

"Tomorrow's a big day, Elmo," said Daddy.

"The first day of school!"

Elmo looked worried.

"What's wrong, Elmo?" asked Daddy.

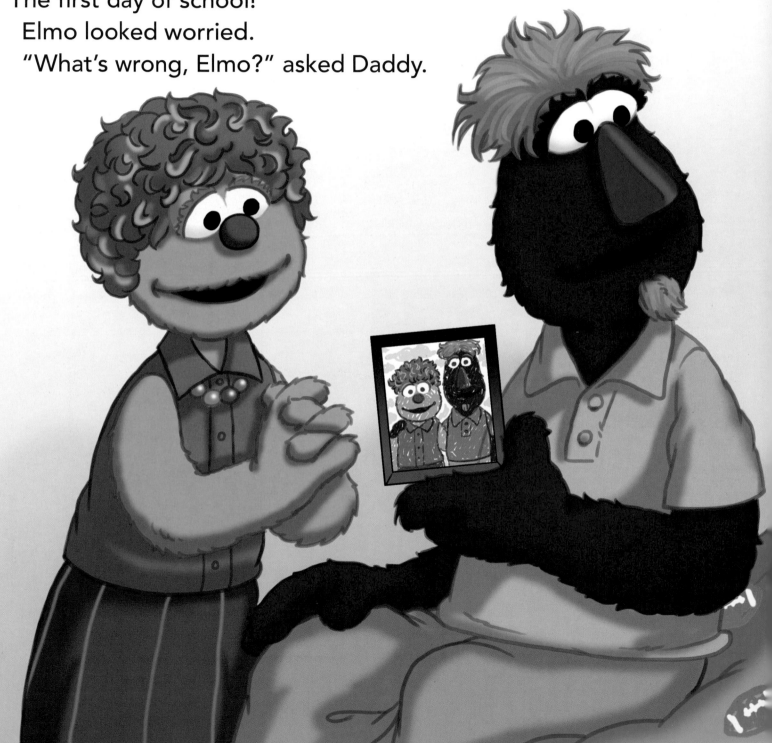

"It's okay to miss us, Elmo," said Daddy as he gave Elmo a big hug. "We'll miss you, too. Mommy and I have a special picture of ourselves, which you can take to school. That way, we'll be with you all day long."

The next morning, Elmo watched as his mom made a sandwich.
"How does this look for your first-day-of-school lunch?" asked Mom.
"It looks good," said Elmo.
"After this, we'll go and make sure your backpack is ready. Okay?"
Elmo looked upset. Mommy asked him what was wrong.

What if . . . ?
What if Elmo has
so much fun that
Elmo doesn't want
to *leave* school?

"Oh, sweetie. Don't worry. That's a good problem to have! But remember that when you come home from school, you have your play date with Cookie Monster. You'll want to be here for that, right?"

"Yes!" said Elmo. "Elmo is so excited!"